GUEST BOOK

It's a boy

Name:
It's a boy

Name:
It's a boy

Name:
It's a boy

Name:
It's a boy

Name:
It's a boy

Name:
It's a boy

Name:
It's a boy

Name:
It's a boy

Name:
It's a boy

Name:
It's a boy

Name:
It's a boy

Name:
It's a boy

Name:
It's a boy

Name:
It's a boy

Name:
It's a boy

Name:
It's a boy

Name:
It's a boy

Name:
It's a boy

Name:
It's a boy

Name:
It's a boy

Name:
It's a boy

Name:
It's a boy

Name:
It's a boy

Name:
It's a boy

Name:
It's a boy

Name:
It's a boy

Name:
It's a boy

Name:
It's a boy

Name:
It's a boy

Name:
It's a boy

Name:
It's a boy

Name:
It's a boy

Name:
It's a boy

Name:
It's a boy

Name:
It's a boy

Name:
It's a boy

Name:
It's a boy

Name:
It's a boy

Name:
It's a boy

Name:
It's a boy

Name:
It's a boy

Name:
It's a boy

Name:
It's a boy

Name:
It's a boy

Name:
It's a boy

Name:
It's a boy

Name:
It's a boy

Name:
It's a boy

Name:
It's a boy

Name:
It's a boy

Name:
It's a boy

Name:
It's a boy

Name:
It's a boy

Name:
It's a boy

Name:
It's a boy

Name:
It's a boy

Name:
It's a boy

Name:
It's a boy

Name:
It's a boy

Name:
It's a boy

Name:
It's a boy

Name:
It's a boy

Name:
It's a boy

Name:
It's a boy

Name:
It's a boy

Name:
It's a boy

Name:
It's a boy

Name:
It's a boy

Name:
It's a boy

Name:
It's a boy

Name:
It's a boy

Name:
It's a boy

Name:
It's a boy

Name:
It's a boy

Name:
It's a boy

Name:
It's a boy

Name:
It's a boy

Name:
It's a boy

Name:
It's a boy

Name:

Name:
It's a boy

Name:
It's a boy

Name:
It's a boy

Name:
It's a boy

Name:
It's a boy

Name:
It's a boy

Name:
It's a boy

Name:
It's a boy

Name:
It's a boy

Name:
It's a boy

Name:
It's a boy

Name:
It's a boy

Name:
It's a boy

Name:
It's a boy

Name:
It's a boy

Name:
It's a boy

Name:
It's a boy

Name:
It's a boy

Name:
It's a boy

Name:
It's a boy